Close-up Continents

Mapping Australasia and Antarctica

Paul Rockett

✦

with artwork by Mark Ruffle

W

FRANKLIN WATTS

Franklin Watts
First published in Great Britain in 2016 by
The Watts Publishing Group

Copyright © The Watts Publishing
Group 2016

Executive editor: Adrian Cole
Series design and illustration: Mark Ruffle
www.rufflebrothers.com

Picture credits:
Jon Arnold Images/Alamy: 27b; EPA/Ettore
Ferrari/Alamy: 23; Jinny Goodman/Alamy:
19b; Nick Haslam/Alamy: 25t; G Brad
Lewis/Science Faction/Corbis: 15t;
Julie McNeil/CC Wikimedia: 9c; Johan
Mollerberg/Dreamstime: 24t; NASA/
Johnson Space Center: 14b; NOAA: 29b;
Chris Rainier/Corbis: 19c; Percy Smith/
CC Wikimedia: 8c; George Steinmetz/
Corbis: 21t; Jim Sugar/Corbis: 17t;
Stephen Tappley/Dreamstime: 17b;
Travelling-Light/Dreamstime: 18b;
Travelscape Images/Alamy: 24c;
CC Wikimedia: 06-07, 9c, 22.

Every attempt has been made to
clear copyright. Should there by any
inadvertent omission please apply to the
publisher for rectification.

Dewey number: 919
ISBN: 978 1 4451 4120 6

Printed in Malaysia

Franklin Watts
An imprint of Hachette Children's Group
Part of The Watts Publishing Group
Carmelite House
50 Victoria Embankment
London EC4Y 0DZ

An Hachette UK Company.
www.hachette.co.uk

www.franklinwatts.co.uk

Contents

Where is Australasia?

Out of the seven continents of the world, Australasia is the smallest. It's made up of one very large island, Australia, the countries of New Zealand and Papua New Guinea, as well as thousands of small islands in the Pacific Ocean.

Papua New Guinea

Australia

Pacific Ocean

New Zealand

Locating Australasia

We can describe the position of Australasia in relation to the areas of land and water that surround it, as well as by using the points on a compass.

Australasia is between the Indian Ocean and the Pacific Ocean

Australasia is north of Antarctica

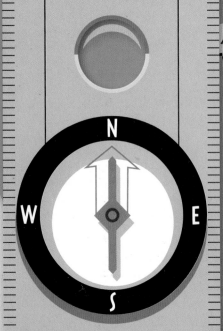

Antarctica

A collection of continents

Some geographers believe there is more than one continent within the area of Australasia.

Australia

They define a continent as being made up of a single landmass and therefore view Australia as a continent.

Zealandia

Others see New Zealand as part of a separate continent called Zealandia. This includes an area of land surrounding New Zealand that is under the sea.

Land area under water ·········

Oceania

Some geographers believe that all of the islands within the central and South Pacific are part of a continent called Oceania. Australia is sometimes included in this group.

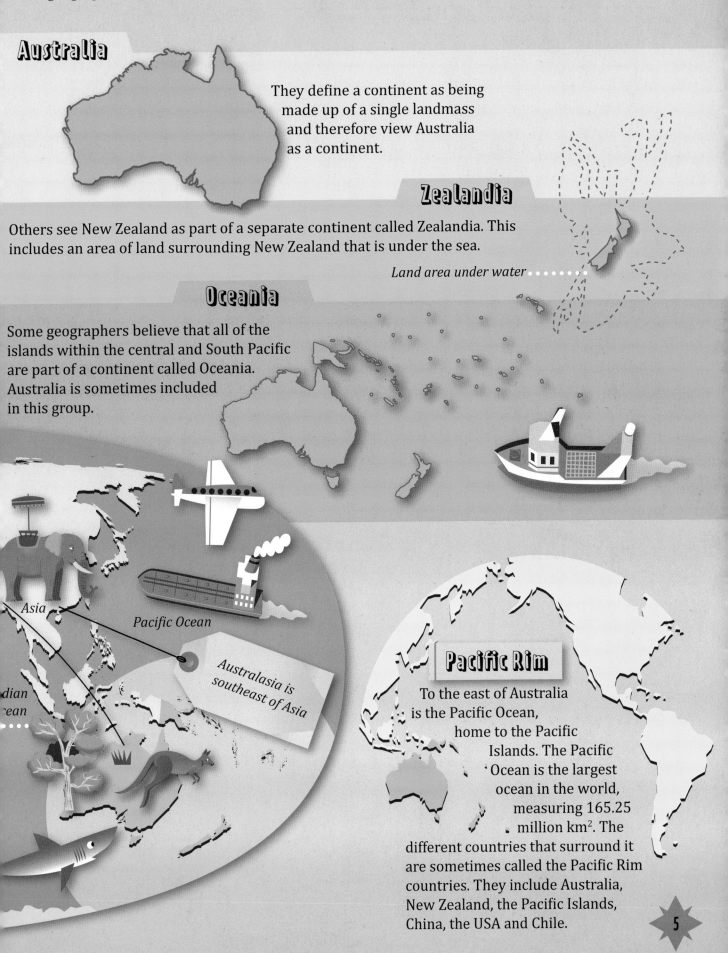

Asia

Pacific Ocean

Australasia is southeast of Asia

dian
cean

Pacific Rim

To the east of Australia is the Pacific Ocean, home to the Pacific Islands. The Pacific Ocean is the largest ocean in the world, measuring 165.25 million km^2. The different countries that surround it are sometimes called the Pacific Rim countries. They include Australia, New Zealand, the Pacific Islands, China, the USA and Chile.

Countries

There are 14 countries in the continent of Australasia, and thousands of small islands. Many of these islands are not independent countries, but are the overseas territory of countries from around the world. These countries are called sovereign states and have an important influence on how the islands are governed.

Northern Mariana Islands
(sovereign state: USA)

Palau

Federated States of Micronesia

Papua New Guinea

Australia

Solomon Islands

New Caledonia
(sovereign state: France)

WA

NT

Qld

SA

NSW

Vic.

Te Ika-a-Māui
(North Island)

Te Waipounamu
(South Island)

Tas.

New Zealand

Australian states

Australia is divided up into seven main states:

NSW = New South Wales
NT = Northern Territory
Qld = Queensland
SA = South Australia
Tas. = Tasmania
Vic. = Victoria
WA = Western Australia

Marshall Islands

Hawaii
(part of the USA)

Kiribati

Nauru

French Polynesia
(sovereign state: France)

Tuvalu

Samoa

Vanuatu

Easter Island
(part of Chile)

Fiji

Tonga

Not all sovereign states are shown. See page 30 for list of Australasian countries.

Cook Islands
(sovereign state: New Zealand)

Pacific Islands

The Australasian islands in the Pacific Ocean are placed into three groups based on their similarities and differences in geography and culture. These are: Polynesia, Micronesia and Melanesia.

Micronesia

There are more than 2,000 islands in the region of Micronesia. The majority are uninhabited and are mainly small low-lying coral islands.

Melanesia

The majority of Pacific islanders live on Melanesian Islands. The largest island and country here is Papua New Guinea; the western part of this island belongs to Indonesia and is part of the continent of Asia.

Polynesia

The islands of Polynesia are spread across a vast area of ocean, stretching from Hawaii in the north to New Zealand in the south and Easter Island in the east. This area is known as the Polynesian Triangle and contains over 1,000 islands.

Early maps and ownership

The original inhabitants of Australasia are thought to have travelled down from different parts of Asia up to 60,000 years ago.

The descendants of those settlers are described as indigenous peoples; in Australia there are the Aborigines, and in New Zealand there are the Maoris. There is also a smaller group, known as the Torres Strait Islanders in the north of Queensland, Australia and in the Melanesian Islands south of Papua New Guinea.

Ocean maps

Early inhabitants of the Marshall Islands, in Micronesia, used stick charts to help navigate around the Pacific Ocean. Made from strips of coconut fibre and shells, these charts mapped parts of the ocean, marking out islands, waves and ocean currents.

Islanders memorised the stick charts before setting out to sea in their canoes.

Aboriginal mapping

Australian Aborigines drew maps with symbols that marked the location of water holes and other landscape features. The maps were usually drawn on the ground, and often included stories that describe the creation of the world, called the Dreamtime. Here are some Aboriginal symbols:

Cliff or sandhill

Water

Water holes connected by running water

Star

Sitting-down place

The European invasion

European explorers arrived in the 16th century. Over the next 300 years, Europe took control of Australasia. Many of the people who live here now are descended from Europeans.

1519–21
Portuguese navigator, Ferdinand Magellan, sails across the Pacific, reaching Guam.

1606
First sighting by a European of northern Australia by Dutch explorer, Willem Janszoon.

1642–5
Dutchman, Abel Tasman, sails round parts of Australia and visits New Zealand, New Guinea, Tonga and Fiji. He names Australia New Holland.

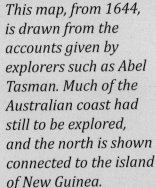

This map, from 1644, is drawn from the accounts given by explorers such as Abel Tasman. Much of the Australian coast had still to be explored, and the north is shown connected to the island of New Guinea.

1768
English explorer Captain James Cook begins a voyage around the Pacific. He lands at Botany Bay, Australia, in 1770. Cook made three voyages exploring Australasia.

1788
The British claim control of the eastern side of Australia, calling it New South Wales. They send a boat of convicts off to Australia to be housed in Port Jackson (Sydney).

1840
In New Zealand, Maori chiefs sign the Treaty of Waitangi, an agreement between the British government and Maori tribes.

1907
New Zealand is granted independence from Britain.

1901
Australia becomes independent from British rule.

1860s–72
Series of battles between British settlers and the Maori over land and colonial control.

Colonial control

The Pacific Islands have been controlled by the Dutch, Spanish, British, French, German, Japanese and US governments. The islands eventually began to gain independence, starting with Samoa in 1962 to Palau in 1994.

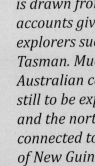

Climate

Australasia enjoys a warm climate, with bright sunshine and cool breezes by the coast. However the weather in this continent creates dry deserts and humid rainforests and can also trigger destructive fires, storms and devastating droughts.

Australasia has four climate zones:

tropical humid
dry
Mediterranean
marine west coast

Each zone experiences different weather conditions that shape their wildlife and the lifestyles of those who live there.

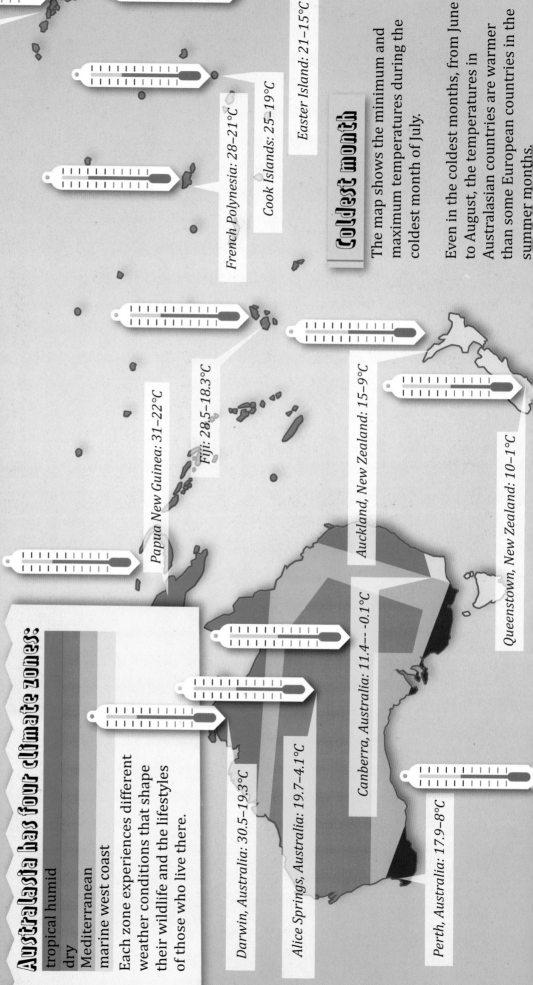

Hawaii: 31.1–20.6°C

French Polynesia: 28–21°C

Cook Islands: 25–19°C

Easter Island: 21–15°C

Papua New Guinea: 31–22°C

Fiji: 28.5–18.3°C

Auckland, New Zealand: 15–9°C

Queenstown, New Zealand: 10–1°C

Darwin, Australia: 30.5–19.3°C

Alice Springs, Australia: 19.7–4.1°C

Canberra, Australia: 11.4–-0.1°C

Perth, Australia: 17.9–8°C

Coldest month

The map shows the minimum and maximum temperatures during the coldest month of July.

Even in the coldest months, from June to August, the temperatures in Australasian countries are warmer than some European countries in the summer months.

Climate Catastrophes

Bushfires

Australia has a largely hot and dry climate. During the hottest months of the year, December to February, it often experiences heat waves and droughts. This causes the forests and grasslands to become extremely dry. The dry vegetation can catch fire easily and the fire spreads quickly. These are known as bushfires.

TOTAL BAN ON ALL BURNING, BARBEQUES AND INCINERATORS
CATASTROPHIC
EXTREME
SEVERE
VERY HIGH
HIGH
LOW

This is a fire danger chart used to warn of bushfires. The ratings are based on temperature, wind speed and humidity, and dryness of vegetation.

El Niño

The climate of the Pacific Islands is influenced by changing wind pressures and temperatures that cross over the Pacific Ocean. Sometimes extreme weather conditions occur, such as an El Niño, causing dramatic changes to a country's climate.

Normal year

Normally, strong winds blow warm surface water west across the Pacific Ocean, towards Australasia. This increases rainfall and encourages tropical rainforest conditions.

Pacific Ocean

El Niño year

An El Niño occurs when the wind changes direction and the warm surface water is blown east, towards the coast of South America.

This change often causes extreme weather, bringing heavy storms and cyclones to South America, while leaving areas of Australasia affected by drought.

Pacific Ocean

Key:

➡ = strong ocean currents and winds

- - -▶ = weak ocean currents and winds

Wildlife

The vast open landscape in Australia and the dense island forests in the Pacific are home to some of the world's oddest and most dangerous wildlife.

BEWARE!

An Inland taipan's bite contains enough venom to kill around 100 people. A blue-ring octopus carries around enough venom to kill 26 people. The saltwater crocodile kills one to two people a year. The red-back spider's bite will leave you with a burning fever.

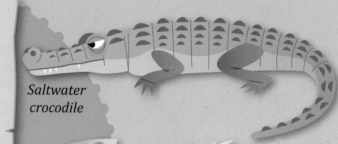

Saltwater crocodile

Inland taipan

Redback spider

Blue-ringed octopus

Kookaburra

Dingo

Eucalyptus tree

Animals from Europe

European settlers brought new animals to Australia, including horses to ride and animals for farming, such as sheep, cows and rabbits. Rabbits escaped into the wild and quickly grew in number – they are now viewed as a major pest.

Marsupials

Marsupials are mammals with pouches which they use to carry their young. They only live in Australasia and the Americas. The majority, around 200 species, are found in Australia and Papua New Guinea.

Marsupials include the kangaroo, koala, numbat, wombat, bilbie, possum and Tasmanian devil.

Wombat

Kangaroo

Koala

Monotremes

Monotremes are mammals that lay eggs. They are only found in Australia and Papua New Guinea. There are two kinds of monotremes in the world: the echidna and the platypus. Both look like a strange combination of different creatures: the platypus has a duck-like bill and beaver-like tail, whereas the echidna has long spines over its back and a long snout like an anteater's.

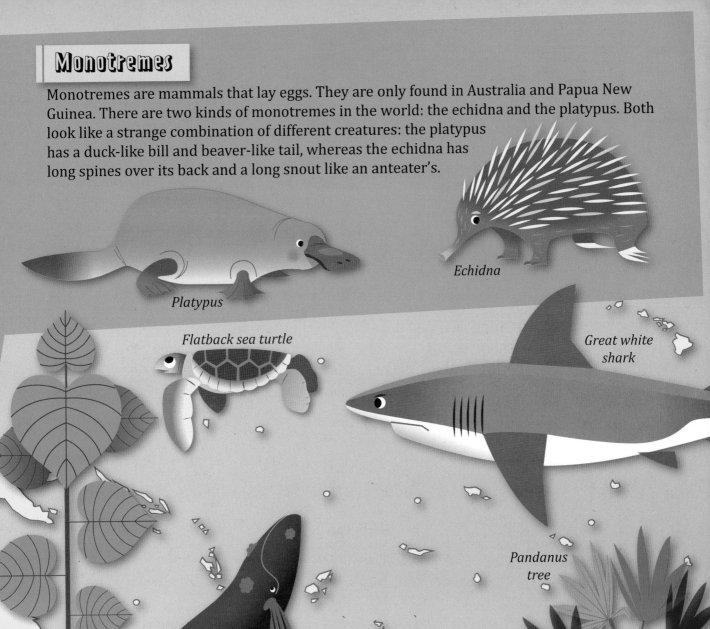

Echidna

Platypus

Flatback sea turtle

Great white shark

Gympie Gympie (stinging tree)

Humpback whale

Pandanus tree

Powelliphanta

Flightless birds

There are more flightless birds in New Zealand than anywhere else in the world. They include kiwis, takahē, kakapo and penguins.

The kiwi only lives in New Zealand.

Tasmanian devil

The Tasmanian devil is only the size of a small dog, but is the largest carnivorous marsupial. Its name comes from the fact that it only lives on Tasmania and makes piercing shrieks and screams.

Emu

13

Natural landmarks

Australasia is still largely uninhabited. Vast deserts, steamy rainforests, coral reefs, fiery volcanoes and high mountains can all be found on the continent.

Great Barrier Reef

The Great Barrier Reef is the largest living structure on Earth. It's made up of billions of coral, stretching over 2,000 km in length. It's one of the richest ecosystems on Earth, home to thousands of different species of marine life, including molluscs, parrotfish and sharks.

Uluru

Near the centre of Australia is the iconic giant sandstone monolith, Uluru. It's 348 m high, and changes colour in the sunlight during the day, glowing red at dawn and sunset.

It's a landmark that holds particular importance to local Aboriginal peoples, featuring in many of their creation stories.

Atolls

The Pacific Ocean is home to the largest number of atolls in the world. These are flat coral islands that encircle a shallow body of water, known as a lagoon. They form around the remains of sunken islands that were created by the build-up of lava from underwater volcanoes.

Great Barrier Reef

Great Dividing Range

Coral Sea Island

Pinnacles Desert

Darling River

Murray River

Blue Mountains

Wave Rock

Atafu is an atoll that is part of the islands of Tokelau.

Hawaii

The island of Hawaii is made up of five volcanoes. These include one of the largest active volcanoes in the world, Maunu Loa, measuring 4,169 m in height. It also has the world's tallest mountain, the dormant volcano Mauna Kea. It measures 10,203 m up from the seabed, although only 4,205 m of this is above sea level.

Hawaii

Pu'u 'Ula'ula

Mauna Kea

Kohala

Mauna Loa

Kilauea

Marshall Islands

Kiribati Islands

The volcanic activity on Hawaii is causing the island to grow in size. Lava from the Kilauea volcano flows into the Pacific Ocean and cools to form new land.

ıru   Banabu

Caroline Island

○ = High island rock

◗ = Atoll coral reef

Tuvali

Tokelau

Makatea

Tuamotu

Niue

Henderson

Ring of Fire

New Zealand's Southern Alps is a mountain range which has formed where the Pacific and Indo-Australian tectonic plates meet. It is also the beginning of the Ring of Fire – a string of 452 volcanoes that are located around the edge of the Pacific Ocean and which form a rough horseshoe shape.

The Ring of Fire volcanoes are some of the most active volcanoes in the world. Here, the edge of the Pacific Plate expands and collides with neighbouring tectonic plates, causing volcanic activity and earthquakes.

Mount Taranaki

Rotorua thermal geysers

Southern Alps

Aoraki

Ring of Fire

15

Manmade landmarks

The manmade landmarks in Australasia show off the amazing building skills of people in the past and up to the modern day.

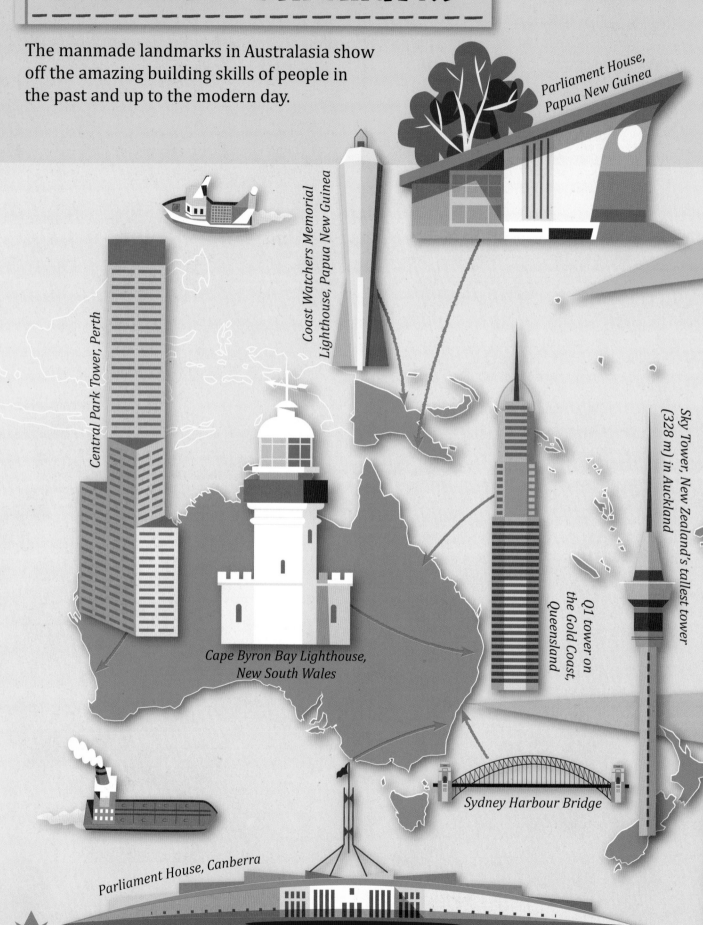

Parliament House, Papua New Guinea

Coast Watchers Memorial Lighthouse, Papua New Guinea

Central Park Tower, Perth

Sky Tower, New Zealand's tallest tower (328 m) in Auckland

Q1 tower on the Gold Coast, Queensland

Cape Byron Bay Lighthouse, New South Wales

Sydney Harbour Bridge

Parliament House, Canberra

Nan Madol

Nan Madol (below) is an ancient ruined city that lies off the east coast of the island of Pohnpei, part of the Federated States of Micronesia. Between 500 CE and 1500 CE, people there constructed royal palaces, tombs and other buildings, using heavy stone and coral. No one is sure how the stones got there. According to local legend they were flown in by black magic!

0   100 200M

Nan Madol was the centre of a ruling empire that had disappeared by the time the Europeans arrived.

Ha'amonga 'a Maui, Tonga

Tiki Takai'i, French Polynesia

Moai

Easter Island is famous for its giant statues that stare blankly across its landscape. They are called *moai* and were carved by the Rapa Nui people who lived on the island. They were made from around 1000 CE until the late 1600s.

It's thought that the moai were created to represent powerful chiefs, keeping watch over their people.

= Moai

Easter Island

Sydney Opera House

The most famous building in Australia is the Sydney Opera House. It was designed by Danish architect, Jørn Utzon. Concerts, plays and ballets are performed here, as well as operas.

The sails of great ships inspired the design of the shell-like roofs. The design connects the buildings to its location alongside Sydney Harbour.

The majority of the Easter Island figures are carved from hardened volcanic ash, and all but seven face inland.

Settlements

Most of Australasia's settlements have been built along the coastline. It's cooler here than it is inland, and it's also the place where settlers would have first arrived, building their camps and colonies near to where their canoes and ships docked.

Indigenous land

In 1995, the Indigenous Land Corporation was set up in Australia. It helps Aboriginal communities regain control of and manage their land. This land is kept clear of cattle farming and mining industries. Here, Aboriginal peoples can live alongside the natural environment, practising the traditions of their ancestors.

Perth

Adelaide

= Major cities

= Inner regional Australia

= Outer regional Australia

= Very remote Australia

= Areas of indigenous land

Perth

Perth is the largest city in Western Australia and one of the most isolated cities in the world. The next closest big city, Adelaide, is 2,104 km away.

Huli tribe

The Huli people live in the Tari rainforest in the Southern Highlands of Papua New Guinea. Their way of life has changed little since they first had contact with Europeans in 1935.

Huli men and women live in separate huts. The men are hunter-gatherers whereas the women tend gardens, growing vegetables such as sweet potatoes and yams. The women also share their homes with pigs, which are used as a form of currency.

The Huli people still wear traditional outfits for special occasions. Faces are painted and the men wear wigs made from their own hair, decorated with feathers from tropical birds.

Christchurch

New Zealand experiences thousands of small earthquakes each year – most are minor causing small tremors. However, when big earthquakes strike they can cause terrible damage to homes and cities.

A major earthquake hit New Zealand's second-largest city, Christchurch, in 2011. The force was greater than anything the city had previously experienced; it destroyed around 60 per cent of the city centre and killed 185 people. It took two years to make the centre safe, and reopen buildings to the public.

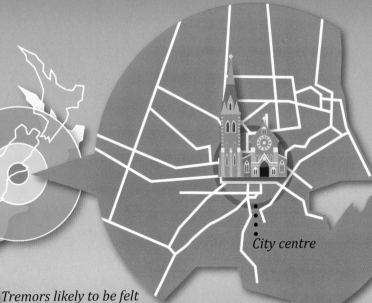

City centre

Tremors likely to be felt

Possible contents damage

Possible structural damage to buildings

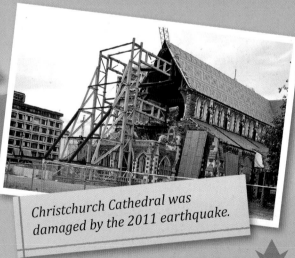

Christchurch Cathedral was damaged by the 2011 earthquake.

Industry

Farms, big and small, are essential for food and trade within the islands of Australasia. The islands' isolation and natural beauty make them popular with tourists, and many local people have jobs connected to tourism. Mining and manufacturing are also big business for the larger islands.

Imports and exports

Australasia's nearest continental neighbour is Asia. The short distance between them means goods do not have very far to travel.

The blue arrows around the Pacific Ocean show the route a freight ship from Asia takes as it delivers and picks up goods from ports around Australasia.

Imports
The main goods Australasia imports from Asia include computers, televisions, toys, games, sporting goods and furniture.

Lihir, Papua New Guinea

Ooldea

Loongana

Indian Pacific railway

Exports
The main exports from Australia are iron, coal, gold and professional services.

Transport connections

To help reach many of the distant places in Australia, there are over 400 airports dotted around the country. There are also major rail networks that transport people and goods across its vast landscape.

The Indian Pacific railway includes the world's longest stretch of dead-straight railway track. The line travels straight for 478 km between Loongana and Ooldea.

Main industries in Australasia

Crops:
- 🍎 Fruit
- Maize
- Oats
- Rice
- Sugar
- Vines
- Wheat

Industry:
- Mining
- Fishing
- Car industry
- Electronics
- Tourism

Livestock:
- Cattle
- Sheep

Lihir mine

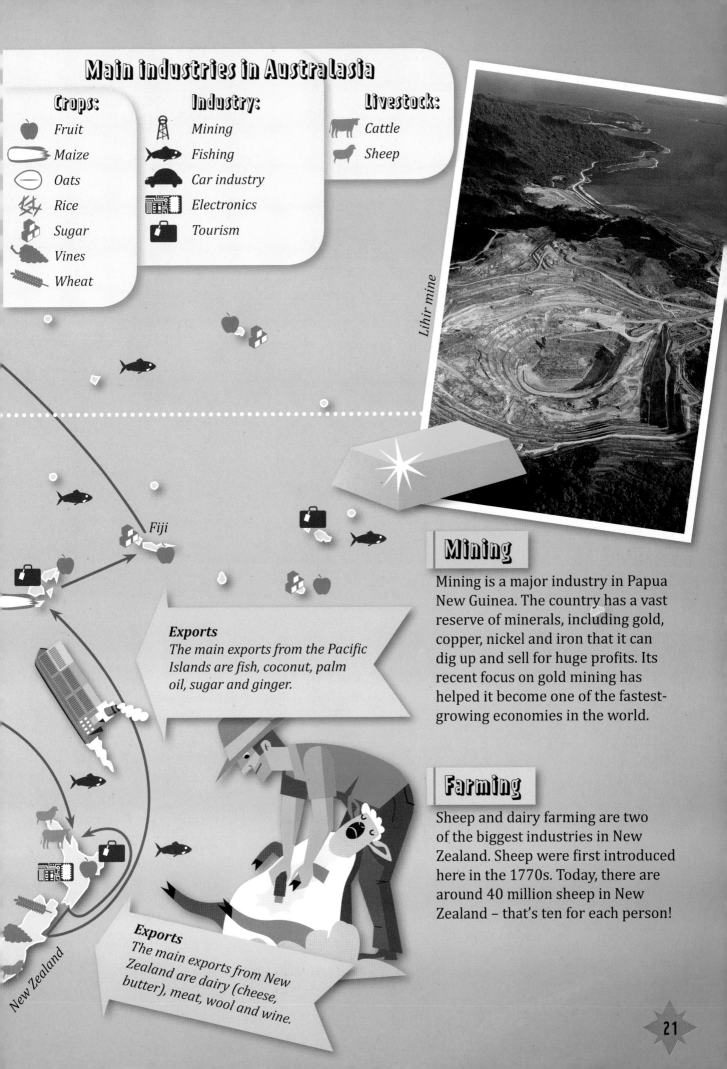

Fiji

Exports
The main exports from the Pacific Islands are fish, coconut, palm oil, sugar and ginger.

New Zealand

Exports
The main exports from New Zealand are dairy (cheese, butter), meat, wool and wine.

Mining

Mining is a major industry in Papua New Guinea. The country has a vast reserve of minerals, including gold, copper, nickel and iron that it can dig up and sell for huge profits. Its recent focus on gold mining has helped it become one of the fastest-growing economies in the world.

Farming

Sheep and dairy farming are two of the biggest industries in New Zealand. Sheep were first introduced here in the 1770s. Today, there are around 40 million sheep in New Zealand – that's ten for each person!

Sport

Australasia takes part in many international sporting events, producing top-ranking rugby players, and swimming and tennis stars. It's also home to their own sports, including surfing and a different type of football, known as Australian Rules Football.

Surfing

Polynesians were known for their outstanding abilities in sea navigation as they travelled around the ocean in small boats and canoes. They were also experts at surfing, a sport that existed here a long time before the Europeans arrived. It was most popular in Hawaii, where everyone enjoyed it, from warrior chiefs to farmers, women, children and even grandparents.

Hawaii

Rugby

New Zealand's national rugby union team, nicknamed the All Blacks, are one of the top-ranking teams in the world.

Before each match they perform a traditional Maori dance, called the Haka. This dance includes chanting, grunting and feet stamping. It was originally performed by warriors before going into battle.

Australian Rules Football

Australian Rules Football is a contact sport that is believed to have begun in Melbourne, in 1859.

Quick rule guide:

- played with a ball shaped like a rugby ball;

- two teams of 18 players;

- points scored by kicking the ball between two tall goal posts;

- players may run and carry the ball the entire length of the pitch, provided they bounce or touch the ball on the ground at least once every 15 m;

- the ball can be kicked or handballed (a handball is when the ball is held in one hand and punched with the fist of the other hand).

The All Blacks performing the Haka.

Rugby is also hugely popular among many of the Pacific Island nations, with top teams from Tonga, Fiji and Samoa.

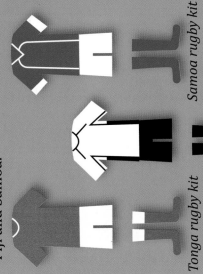

Tonga rugby kit

Fiji rugby kit

Samoa rugby kit

Bungee jumping

New Zealanders and thrill-seeking tourists have been bungee jumping here since the mid-1980s. The participant jumps off a high ledge, around 400 m high, with an elastic rope (bungee) attached to their ankles. When the bungee is fully stretched, the person springs back up.

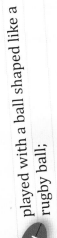

Culture

Australasia has a rich multi-cultural society. Settlers from Europe, Asia, and the USA brought their traditions, beliefs and culture with them, but the cultures of the indigenous peoples are an important part of the continent's heritage and continue to be celebrated today.

Prize winners

The Nobel Prize is an international award given to those who have produced work that has benefitted humankind. Australia has produced 15 Nobel Prize winners, which is the highest number per head of population of any country; New Zealand has produced three. Most of these winners worked in science or medicine.

Aboriginal culture is strongly connected to the land. Artwork is often painted onto objects from the landscape, such as rocks and sheets of bark (above).

Aboriginal culture

Australian Aboriginal culture is one of the longest-surviving cultures in the world. It lives on through ceremonies of dancing and singing and the visual arts. Objects, such as the didgeridoo and the boomerang (below), have become internationally known emblems of their culture. The demand for artefacts and artwork provides Aboriginal communities with a source of income.

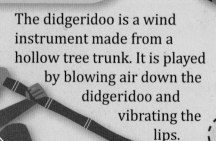

The didgeridoo is a wind instrument made from a hollow tree trunk. It is played by blowing air down the didgeridoo and vibrating the lips.

The boomerang is a wooden tool used in hunting. A returnable boomerang is designed to return to the thrower.

Tattoos

The word 'tattoo' comes from the Tahitian term *tatau*. In Tahiti and other Polynesian islands, tattooing is an important part of tribal culture. In the past, Samoan boys were tattooed as a sign that they'd reached adulthood, whereas in Fiji this act was more common for young women.

Patterns vary from island to island. Designs include images from nature, such as worms and starfish. Many of these designs are popular around the world today and still remain important and symbolic for the descendants of the indigenous Polynesians.

Samoa

Tahiti

Fiji

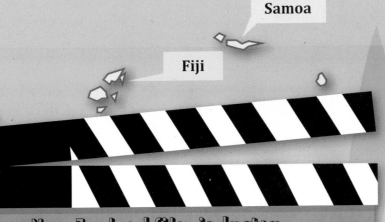

New Zealand film industry

New Zealand has become a top destination for making blockbuster movies. The country has a diverse landscape offering scenery that suits fantasy films, such as the *Lord of the Rings* trilogy. It also has highly talented special effects companies, directors and production teams.

New Zealand

Food and drink

Across Australasia, people enjoy a great variety of local foods. There are foods from ancient indigenous cultures, foods introduced during colonisation and foods brought over by more recent settlers. Chefs continue to develop this rich food tradition.

Noodles

Sago

Bush tucker

Bush tucker refers to food that can be sourced by someone living off the land. This ranges from the witchetty grubs, green ants and snakes eaten by indigenous Aboriginal people to the campsite foods of colonial settlers.
These include:

Damper
(bread baked in the ashes of a camp fire or in a cap oven)

Bush oysters
(lamb or cattle testicles)

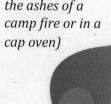

Paddy melon
(a small marsupial)

Meat pie

Anzac biscuits

Queensland

Pavlova

Barbecue

VEGEMITE

Yabbies

Lamingtons

Lamingtons are a dessert named after Lord Lamington, the Governor of Queensland from 1896–1901. There are many stories telling how the cake came about. One story tells of the Lamingtons paying a visit to an ordinary household in the outback. In a panic to impress her important guests, the host quickly chopped up a stale sponge cake and dipped it in chocolate and shredded coconut.

Pacific Rim cuisine

The different foods and methods of cooking from around the countries and islands of the Pacific Rim are often combined. This is known as Pacific Rim cuisine, where Asian spices and noodles are mixed with traditional produce from Hawaii or Guam. These foods are particularly popular in Australia and New Zealand. It reflects the effect immigration has had on creating a wider choice of food on the menu.

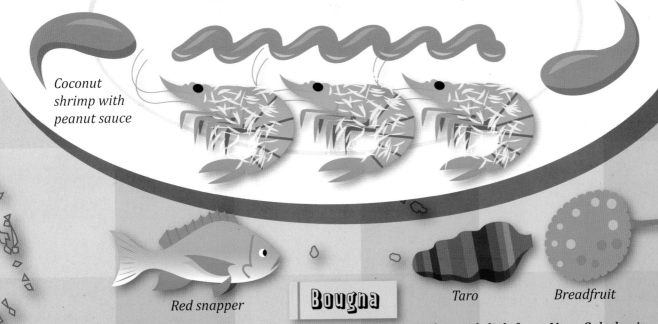

Coconut shrimp with peanut sauce

Red snapper

Taro

Breadfruit

Bougna

Bougna is a traditional dish from New Caledonia. It involves layers of food wrapped in a large bundle of banana leaves that are cooked in an underground oven for two hours. At the bottom are yams and taro, with bananas, plantains or breadfruit placed over these and fish or meat on top.

Roast lamb

Wine

The warm climates of the Southern Hemisphere have helped to make both Australia and New Zealand perfect places for growing grapevines and producing award-winning wines.

This woman is preparing her bougna dish.

Kiwi fruit

27

Where is Antarctica?

Antarctica is the fifth largest continent in the world, measuring 13,800,000 km². It sits at the very bottom of the Southern Hemisphere and is home to the South Pole. Its name 'Antarctica' means 'opposite of Arctic'.

Human inhabitants

Antarctica does not belong to any one country, although some countries have claimed parts of it as their own territory.

No one lives on Antarctica permanently, but approximately 5,000 scientists and support staff stay there for limited periods of time. They work in research stations that are maintained by various countries, including Japan, New Zealand, Argentina, USA, Russia and the UK.

First human contact

No one is entirely sure who was the first person to set foot on Antarctica. Some think that it was an Anglo-American called Captain John Davis. He's thought to have arrived at Hughes Bay to hunt for seals.

🚩 = Research station

Australia

Antarctica

Giant cranch squid

Antarctic hair grass

Antarctic fur seal

Ross Ice Shelf

Ice shelves are floating sheets of ice that are connected to a landmass. The largest in Antarctica is the Ross Ice Shelf, which is roughly the size of France.

—— Amundsen route
—— Scott route

Mount Vinson is the highest mountain in Antarctica, measuring 4,892 m in height.

South Pole

Emperor penguins

Albatross

Hughes Bay

Elephant seal

Race to the South Pole

In December 1911, two expeditions set out to see who could reach the South Pole first. One was a Norwegian team, led by Roald Amundsen; the other was a British team, led by Captain Robert Falcon Scott.

They each took different routes, with Amundsen reaching the South Pole first, on 14 December 1911. Scott's team finally arrived on 25 January 1912. Sadly, Scott's team never made it back to base camp, perishing in a blizzard on their return journey.

Polar desert

Antarctica has a polar desert landscape. It's too cold and windy for trees and shrubs to grow here, but there are low-growing lichens, grasses and mosses. Seals and penguins survive well as they have thick fatty layers of skin that help keep them warm and there is plenty of food to catch in the sea.

Ozone is a colourless gas that absorbs harmful ultraviolet rays that come from the Sun. The ozone layer protects the Earth from these rays.

The hole in the ozone layer has caused ice shelves in Antarctica to melt, affecting its ecosystem. Until recent changes in pollution laws the hole was getting larger, however it's now thought to be getting smaller.

The ozone hole

The Earth shown right is displayed as a thermal map; it's showing us the amount of ozone in the Earth's atmosphere over Antarctica. The purple and blue areas are where there is the least ozone (the ozone hole) and the yellows and greens are where there is more ozone.

Members of Roald Amundsen's expedition at the South Pole.

COUNTRY	SIZE SQ KM	POPULATION	CAPITAL CITY	MAIN LANGUAGES
Australia	7,741,220	22,751,014	Canberra	English
New Zealand	267,710	4,438,393	Wellington	English, Maori, NZ Sign Language
Polynesia:				
Samoa	2,831	197,773	Apia	Samoan, English
Tonga	747	106,501	Nuku'alofa	Tongan, English
Tuvalu	26	10,869	Funafuti	Tuvaluan, English
Melanesia:				
Papua New Guinea	462,840	6,672,429	Port Moresby	Hiri Motu, Tok Pisin, English
Fiji	18,274	909,389	Suva	English, Fijian, Fiji Hindi
Solomon Islands	28,896	622,469	Honiara	English, Melanesian pidgin
Vanuata	12,189	272,264	Port-Vila	Bislama, French, English
Micronesia:				
Federated States of Micronesia	702	105,216	Palikir	English (official)
Kiribati	811	105,711	South Tarawa	English, Gilbertese, I-Kiribati
Marshall Islands	181	72,191	Majuro	Marshallese, English
Palau	459	21,265	Ngerulmud, Melekeok State	English, Palauan
Nauru	21	9,540	Yaren (largest settlement)	Nauruan, English

Glossary

atoll
an island that is made of coral and shaped like a ring

bushfire
a fire in a forest or area of scrubland that spreads quickly

carnivorous
the description of an animal that eats the flesh of animals

climate
average weather conditions in a particular area

colony
an area of land that is under political control and occupation of another country

convict
a person serving a prison sentence for having committed a criminal offence

currency
a form of money used in different countries and continents, such as the euro or the US dollar

drought
a prolonged period of low rainfall leading to a shortage of water

export
goods or services sold to another country

import
to bring in goods to sell from abroad

indigenous peoples
communities originating from a particular country or region that have lived there long before the invasion and settlement of a foreign society, such as the Aborigines in Australia

marsupial
a mammal with a pouch in which the mother carries her young, such as kangaroos and koalas

monolith
a very large single block of stone

monotreme
mammals that can lay eggs, like the platypus

navigate
plan and direct the course of a ship or other forms of transport by using instruments, such as a compass, and maps

ocean currents
seawater moving from one location to another, driven by wind, differences in water density and rising and falling tides

outback
remote and usually uninhabited areas of land, such as the inland regions of Australia

Southern Hemisphere
section of the Earth that is south of the Equator

sovereign state
a country with territories abroad that it may not directly govern but holds powers and influence that oversee how the territory is run

species
living things that contain shared characteristics, e.g. human beings

tectonic plates
large slow-moving sections of the Earth's surface

thermal geysers
springs of naturally hot water that intermittently send hot columns of water and steam into the air

tremors
a shaking movement that happens underground, usually before an earthquake

Index